BLOOD TYPE O FOOD LIST

LORENE PEACHEY

Copyright © 2024 by Lorene Peachey

All rights reserved.

No part of this publication may be reproduced, stored in a retrieval system, or transmitted, in any form or by any means, electronic, mechanical, photocopying, recording or otherwise, without the prior written permission of the copyright holder.

This book is sold subject to the condition that it shall not, by way of trade or otherwise, be lent, re-sold, hired out or otherwise circulated without the publisher's prior consent in any form of binding or cover other than that in which it is published and without a similar condition including this condition being imposed on the subsequent purchaser.

DISCLAIMER

The content within this book reflects my thoughts, experiences, and beliefs. It is meant for informational and entertainment purposes. While I have taken great care to provide accurate information, I cannot guarantee the absolute correctness or applicability of the content to every individual or situation. Please consult with relevant professionals for advice specific to your needs.

TO GAIN ACCESS TO MORE BOOK BY THE AUTHOR SCAN THE QR CODE

TABLE OF CONTENTS

INTRODUCTION...1

CHAPTER 1 7

Overview of Blood Type O 7

Understanding the Importance of Tailored Nutrition for Blood Type O: 7

CHAPTER 2 11

Blood Type O Characteristics..11

Physical Traits:.. 11

Personality Traits: 12

Metabolic Considerations: 12

Exercise Preferences: 13

Dietary Considerations: 13

CHAPTER 3 15

Protein...15

CHAPTER 4 21

Vegetables 21

CHAPTER 5 25

Fruits 25

CHAPTER 6 29

Dairy and Alternatives **29**

CHAPTER 7 ....**33**

Foods to Limit or Avoid **33**

CHAPTER 8 ....**37**

Grocery Shopping Guide **37**

Reading Food Labels: Key Considerations: 40

CONCLUSION **43**

Bonus CHAPTER 1 ....**46**

healthy blood type O recipes **46**

Bonus CHAPTER 2 ....**57**

Exercise recommendation **57**

INTRODUCTION

In the quiet corners of my cozy kitchen, amidst the aroma of simmering spices and the clinking of utensils, I discovered a passion that would become the heartbeat of my existence – the art and science of tailoring nutrition to the intricate dance of blood types. Hello, dear reader, I am Lorene Peachey, a devoted nutritionist who has spent over two and a half decades unraveling the mysteries of blood type-based diets. As you delve into the pages of this book, join me on a journey that transcends mere culinary exploration; it's a voyage through the very essence of life and well-being.

My odyssey into the world of blood type nutrition began with a simple question: Could the key to optimal health lie within the unique composition of our blood? In pursuit of this query, my life took on a thrilling purpose – a purpose that fueled countless hours of research, experimentation, and a relentless quest for understanding.

Picture this: a kitchen adorned with shelves of vibrant ingredients, each carefully selected to align with the specific needs of blood type O individuals. As I crafted delectable recipes and explored the vast palette of nature's bounty, I couldn't help but marvel at the profound impact these choices had on overall health.

Let me pose a question to you, dear reader: Have you ever considered that the foods you consume could be the key to unlocking a life of boundless energy, enhanced vitality, and lasting well-being? The answer, I discovered, lies not in generic diets but in the unique blueprint imprinted within our blood.

As the pages unfold, I invite you to reflect on the daily choices you make. How does your body respond to the fuel you provide it? Can a simple shift in your dietary habits unleash a cascade of positive changes? The emotional and physical well-being of countless individuals, whose lives have been transformed through blood type O-centric nutrition, bears testimony to the affirmative.

Now, let's delve into the heart of the matter – the undeniable benefits of embracing a blood type O food list. Imagine a life where your energy levels surge, your digestion dances with joy, and your immune system stands as an unyielding fortress against ailments. This is not a mere fantasy; it's the promise embedded in the very fabric of a diet tailored to your blood type.

In the world of blood type O, the benefits extend far beyond physical well-being. Picture waking up each morning with a sense of purpose, a spring in your step that transcends the mundane. Your relationship with food becomes a celebration, a harmonious dance between nourishment and pleasure.

Now, let me share a secret with you, one that goes beyond the realms of nutritional science. It's the magic that happens when you align your diet with your blood type – a profound connection that nourishes not just your body but your spirit. The foods you consume become a symphony, each note resonating with the melody of your unique biology.

But, my dear reader, the converse is also true. As we embark on this journey, let us acknowledge the dangers that lurk in the shadows of uninformed choices. Have you ever considered the consequences of consuming foods that are incompatible with your blood type? The toll it takes on your energy, your mood, and the intricate balance of your body?

Indulge me for a moment. Picture a world where every bite you take is a step towards a healthier, more vibrant you. Now contrast that with the image of a life dictated by foods that clash with your blood type – a life marred by fatigue, digestive woes, and the silent erosion of vitality. It's a stark juxtaposition, isn't it?

As I share the fruits of my 25 years of experience with you, it's not just about presenting a list of foods. It's about empowering you with the knowledge to make choices that resonate with the very core of your being. The danger of neglecting your blood type's dietary needs is not merely theoretical; it's a tangible reality that countless individuals unknowingly face each day.

So, why embark on this journey with me? What sets this blood type O food list apart from the plethora of dietary guides that flood the shelves? The answer lies in the intersection of science and soul, where nutritional wisdom meets the innate wisdom of your body. It's about embracing a lifestyle that transcends the ordinary – a lifestyle that beckons you to not just survive but thrive.

As we navigate the pages ahead, let's unravel the secrets of cooking and dining with purpose. It's not just about the recipes; it's about savoring the journey, relishing each bite as a conscious act of self-love. Join me, not just as a reader but as a fellow traveler on the road to radiant health and profound well-being.

In the following chapters, we will explore the tantalizing array of beneficial foods, the neutral options that offer flexibility, and the cautious avoidance of foods that could disrupt the delicate balance of your blood type O system. But more than that, we will embark on a transformational voyage that goes beyond the kitchen – a journey that transcends the boundaries of nutrition and becomes a celebration of life itself.

Are you ready, dear reader, to step into a world where the choices on your plate are not just meals but moments of empowerment? Let the adventure begin.

Contact the Author

Thank you for reading my book! I would love to hear from you, whether you have feedback, questions, or just want to share your thoughts. Your feedback means a lot to me and helps me improve as a writer.

Please don't hesitate to reach out to me through

lorenepeachey@gmail.com

I look forward to connecting with my readers and appreciate your support in this literary journey. Your thoughts and comments are valuable to me.

CHAPTER 1

OVERVIEW OF BLOOD TYPE O

Blood Type O is one of the four blood types in the ABO blood group system, characterized by the presence of both O antigens on the surface of red blood cells and anti-A and anti-B antibodies in the plasma. Individuals with Blood Type O are often referred to as "universal donors" because their blood can be donated to individuals with any ABO blood type. Beyond its significance in blood transfusions, Blood Type O is associated with specific health considerations, and tailored nutrition based on blood type has gained attention in recent years.

Understanding the Importance of Tailored Nutrition for Blood Type O:

1. **Protein Emphasis:** Blood Type O individuals are often recommended to follow a diet rich in animal protein, such as lean meats and fish. This is thought to align with the presumed ancestral diet of early humans with Blood Type O, which is believed to have been primarily focused on hunting and gathering.

2. **Limited Grains and Dairy:** The recommended diet for Blood Type O typically suggests limiting the consumption of grains and dairy products. It is suggested that these individuals may have a lower tolerance for certain components found in these food groups.

3. **Beneficial Foods:** Certain foods are believed to be particularly beneficial for Blood Type O individuals. These include lean meats, poultry, fish, vegetables, and fruits. Kelp and seafood are often highlighted for their potential health benefits for this blood type.

4. **Exercise Recommendations:** In addition to dietary guidelines, Blood Type O individuals may be encouraged to engage in regular, vigorous physical activity. This is thought to be linked to the supposed ancestral lifestyle associated with this blood type.

5. **Potential Health Implications:** Some proponents of blood type-based nutrition argue that adhering to a diet tailored to one's blood type can lead to improved overall health and a reduced risk of certain conditions. However, it's important to note that scientific evidence supporting these claims is limited, and individual responses to specific diets can vary.

6. **Blood Type and Disease Risk:** Some studies have explored potential associations between blood type and certain health conditions. For example, individuals with Blood Type O may have a lower risk of certain cardiovascular diseases compared to other blood types. However, more research is needed to establish clear causal relationships.

CHAPTER 2

BLOOD TYPE O

CHARACTERISTICS

Blood Type O is associated with specific characteristics, traits, and metabolic considerations that set it apart in the ABO blood group system. While the scientific evidence supporting some of these associations is still a subject of ongoing research, proponents of blood type-based theories suggest certain patterns linked to Blood Type O.

Physical Traits:

- **Mesomorph Build:** Individuals with Blood Type O are often described as having a mesomorph body type, characterized by a naturally muscular and well-defined physique. This trait is linked to the presumed ancestral lifestyle of early humans with Blood Type O, who were believed to have engaged in physically demanding activities like hunting.

- **Strong Immune System:** Some studies suggest that Blood Type O individuals may have a more robust immune system compared to other blood types, potentially providing them with enhanced resistance to certain infections.

Personality Traits:

- **Leadership Qualities:** According to some blood type personality theories, individuals with Blood Type O may possess strong leadership qualities. They are thought to be decisive, organized, and capable of taking charge in various situations.

- **Proactive and Social:** Blood Type O individuals may be characterized as proactive, social, and outgoing. They may thrive in dynamic environments that require quick decision-making.

Metabolic Considerations:

- **High Stomach Acid Production:** Blood Type O individuals are believed to have higher levels of stomach acid, which may contribute to better digestion of animal proteins. This is often cited as a reason for the recommended emphasis on a protein-rich diet.

- **Thyroid Function:** Some proponents of blood type-based nutrition suggest that individuals with Blood Type O may have a more efficient thyroid function. This metabolic aspect is thought to influence the type of foods that are well-tolerated and beneficial for this blood type.

Exercise Preferences:

- **High Energy Levels:** Blood Type O individuals are often associated with high energy levels, and regular, vigorous physical activity is commonly recommended for them. This aligns with the idea that the ancestral lifestyle of Blood Type O involved a significant amount of physical exertion.

Dietary Considerations:

- **Protein-Focused Diet:** It is often suggested that individuals with Blood Type O may benefit from a diet rich in animal protein, including lean meats and fish. This is believed to support their metabolic needs and overall health.

- **Limited Grains and Dairy:** The recommended diet for Blood Type O often involves minimizing the intake of grains and dairy products. It is theorized that certain components in these foods may be less compatible with the metabolism of Blood Type O individuals.

CHAPTER 3

PROTEIN

1. **Grass-Fed Beef:**

   - Nutritional Information (per 3-ounce serving):

     - Protein: 21g

     - Calories: 213

     - Fat: 14g

     - Iron: 2.1mg

2. **Skinless Chicken Breast:**

   - Nutritional Information (per 3-ounce serving):

     - Protein: 26g

     - Calories: 128

     - Fat: 3g

     - Iron: 0.6mg

3. **Salmon:**

- Nutritional Information (per 3-ounce serving):

    - Protein: 22g

    - Calories: 206

    - Fat: 13g

    - Omega-3 Fatty Acids: 1.2g

4. **Turkey:**

- Nutritional Information (per 3-ounce serving):

    - Protein: 25g

    - Calories: 135

    - Fat: 1g

    - Iron: 2mg

5. **Eggs:**

- Nutritional Information (per large egg):

    - Protein: 6g

    - Calories: 72

    - Fat: 5g

    - Iron: 1mg

6. **Tuna:**

- Nutritional Information (per 3-ounce serving, canned in water):

    - Protein: 20g

    - Calories: 99

    - Fat: 0.9g

    - Iron: 1.3mg

7. **Lamb:**

- Nutritional Information (per 3-ounce serving):

    - Protein: 23g

    - Calories: 250

    - Fat: 17g

    - Iron: 2.7mg

8. **Venison:**

- Nutritional Information (per 3-ounce serving):

    - Protein: 23g

    - Calories: 158

    - Fat: 3g

    - Iron: 3.4mg

9. **Quinoa:**

- Nutritional Information (per 1 cup, cooked):

    - Protein: 8g

    - Calories: 222

    - Fat: 4g

    - Iron: 2.8mg

10. **Lentils:**

- Nutritional Information (per 1 cup, cooked):

  - Protein: 18g

  - Calories: 230

  - Fat: 1g

  - Iron: 6.6mg

These protein-rich foods provide a variety of options for individuals with Blood Type O, considering the emphasis on animal proteins in their suggested diet. It's essential to incorporate a balanced mix of proteins, along with other nutrients, to support overall health. Additionally, portion sizes and individual dietary preferences should be taken into account when planning meals.

20 BLOOD TYPE O FOOD LIST

CHAPTER 4

VEGETABLES

1. **Spinach:**

   - Nutritional Information (per 1 cup, raw):

     - Calories: 7

     - Fiber: 0.7g

     - Protein: 0.9g

     - Iron: 0.8mg

2. **Kale:**

   - Nutritional Information (per 1 cup, raw):

     - Calories: 33

     - Fiber: 2.5g

     - Protein: 3.3g

     - Iron: 1.1mg

3. **Broccoli:**

- Nutritional Information (per 1 cup, raw):

    - Calories: 31

    - Fiber: 2.4g

    - Protein: 2.6g

    - Vitamin C: 81mg

4. **Bell Peppers (Red or Green):**

- Nutritional Information (per 1 cup, raw):

    - Calories: 46

    - Fiber: 3.6g

    - Protein: 1.5g

    - Vitamin C: 190mg

5. **Sweet Potatoes:**

- Nutritional Information (per 1 medium-sized, baked):

    - Calories: 103

    - Fiber: 4g

    - Protein: 2.3g

- Vitamin A: 438% DV

6. **Carrots:**

  - Nutritional Information (per 1 cup, raw):

    - Calories: 52

    - Fiber: 3.6g

    - Protein: 1.2g

    - Vitamin A: 428% DV

7. **Asparagus:**

  - Nutritional Information (per 1 cup, raw):

    - Calories: 27

    - Fiber: 2.8g

    - Protein: 2.9g

    - Folate: 70mcg

8. **Zucchini:**

- Nutritional Information (per 1 cup, raw):

    - Calories: 20

    - Fiber: 1g

    - Protein: 1.4g

    - Vitamin C: 21mg

Incorporating a variety of colorful and nutrient-dense vegetables into the diet is crucial for individuals with Blood Type O. These vegetables provide essential vitamins, minerals, and fiber to support overall health and well-being. Adjusting portion sizes and preparation methods based on individual preferences and dietary needs is recommended.

CHAPTER 5

FRUITS

1. **Berries (e.g., Blueberries):**

    - Nutritional Information (per 1 cup, raw):

        - Calories: 84

        - Fiber: 3.6g

        - Vitamin C: 14mg

        - Antioxidants: High

2. **Pineapple:**

    - Nutritional Information (per 1 cup, chunks):

        - Calories: 82

        - Fiber: 2.3g

        - Vitamin C: 79mg

        - Manganese: 1.6mg

3. **Cherries:**

- Nutritional Information (per 1 cup, raw):

    - Calories: 87

    - Fiber: 3g

    - Vitamin C: 9.7mg

    - Anthocyanins: High

4. **Kiwi:**

- Nutritional Information (per medium-sized fruit):

    - Calories: 61

    - Fiber: 2.3g

    - Vitamin C: 71mg

    - Vitamin K: 41mcg

5. **Watermelon:**

- Nutritional Information (per 1 cup, cubes):

    - Calories: 46

    - Fiber: 0.6g

    - Vitamin C: 12.3mg

    - Hydration: High

6. **Apples:**

- Nutritional Information (per medium-sized apple):

  - Calories: 95

  - Fiber: 4g

  - Vitamin C: 14% DV

  - Antioxidants: Moderate

7. **Papaya:**

- Nutritional Information (per 1 cup, chunks):

  - Calories: 59

  - Fiber: 2.5g

  - Vitamin C: 88mg

  - Folate: 53mcg

8. **Grapes (Red or Green):**

- Nutritional Information (per 1 cup):

  - Calories: 104

  - Fiber: 1.4g

  - Vitamin C: 4mg

  - Resveratrol: Present

9. **Oranges:**

- Nutritional Information (per medium-sized orange):

    - Calories: 62

    - Fiber: 3.1g

    - Vitamin C: 69mg

    - Folate: 39mcg

10. **Bananas:**

- Nutritional Information (per medium-sized banana):

    - Calories: 105

    - Fiber: 3.1g

    - Vitamin C: 10mg

    - Potassium: 422mg

Including a variety of fruits in the diet ensures a rich intake of essential vitamins, minerals, and antioxidants. These fruits can be part of a well-balanced diet for individuals with Blood Type O. Adjusting portion sizes based on individual preferences and dietary needs is recommended.

CHAPTER 6

DAIRY AND ALTERNATIVES

Individuals with Blood Type O are generally advised to limit their intake of dairy products. However, some dairy and dairy alternatives may be better tolerated by individuals with this blood type. Here are 10 options along with their approximate nutritional information.

1. **Goat Milk:**

   - Nutritional Information (per 1 cup):

     - Calories: 168

     - Protein: 8.7g

     - Calcium: 327mg

     - Fat: 10g

2. **Sheep Milk Yogurt:**

- Nutritional Information (per 6 ounces):

  - Calories: 150

  - Protein: 10g

  - Calcium: 300mg

  - Fat: 8g

3. **Almond Milk (Unsweetened):**

- Nutritional Information (per 1 cup):

  - Calories: 30

  - Protein: 1g

  - Calcium: 450mg

  - Fat: 2.5g

4. **Coconut Milk (Unsweetened):**

- Nutritional Information (per 1 cup):

  - Calories: 50

  - Protein: 0.5g

  - Calcium: 460mg

  - Fat: 5g

5. **Cashew Cheese:**

- Nutritional Information (per 1 ounce):

  - Calories: 70

  - Protein: 2g

  - Calcium: 0mg

  - Fat: 6g

6. **Lactose-Free Cow's Milk:**

- Nutritional Information (per 1 cup):

  - Calories: 90

  - Protein: 8g

  - Calcium: 300mg

  - Fat: 5g

7. **Greek Yogurt (Full fat):**

- Nutritional Information (per 6 ounces):

  - Calories: 150

  - Protein: 15g

  - Calcium: 200mg

  - Fat: 8g

8. **Oat Milk:**

- Nutritional Information (per 1 cup):

  - Calories: 130

  - Protein: 2g

  - Calcium: 350mg

  - Fat: 2.5g

9. **Soy Milk (Unsweetened):**

- Nutritional Information (per 1 cup):

  - Calories: 80

  - Protein: 7g

  - Calcium: 300mg

  - Fat: 4g

10. **Feta Cheese (Sheep or Goat Milk):**

- Nutritional Information (per 1 ounce):

  - Calories: 75

  - Protein: 4g

  - Calcium: 140mg

  - Fat: 6g

CHAPTER 7

FOODS TO LIMIT OR AVOID

1. **Wheat-Based Products (e.g., Bread, Pasta):**

   - Nutritional Information (per slice of whole wheat bread):

     - Calories: 69

     - Carbohydrates: 12g

     - Protein: 3g

     - Fiber: 2g

2. **Corn-Based Products (e.g., Cornflakes, Corn Tortillas):**

   - Nutritional Information (per cup of cornflakes):

     - Calories: 100

     - Carbohydrates: 24g

     - Protein: 2g

     - Fiber: 0.7g

3. **Dairy Products (e.g., Cow's Milk, Cheese):**

    - Nutritional Information (per 1 cup of whole milk):

        - Calories: 150

        - Protein: 8g

        - Calcium: 276mg

        - Fat: 8g

4. **Kidney Beans:**

    - Nutritional Information (per 1 cup, cooked):

        - Calories: 225

        - Carbohydrates: 40g

        - Protein: 15g

        - Fiber: 11g

5. **Lentils:**

    - Nutritional Information (per 1 cup, cooked):

        - Calories: 230

        - Carbohydrates: 40g

        - Protein: 18g

        - Fiber: 16g

6. **Cabbage:**

  - Nutritional Information (per cup, raw):

    - Calories: 22

    - Carbohydrates: 5g

    - Protein: 1g

    - Fiber: 2g

7. **Brussels Sprouts:**

  - Nutritional Information (per cup, raw):

    - Calories: 38

    - Carbohydrates: 8g

    - Protein: 3g

    - Fiber: 3g

8. **Cauliflower:**

  - Nutritional Information (per cup, raw):

    - Calories: 27

    - Carbohydrates: 5g

    - Protein: 2g

    - Fiber: 3g

9. **Eggplant:**

- Nutritional Information (per cup, cooked):

    - Calories: 35

    - Carbohydrates: 8g

    - Protein: 1g

    - Fiber: 3g

10. **Mushrooms:**

- Nutritional Information (per cup, raw):

    - Calories: 15

    - Carbohydrates: 2g

    - Protein: 2g

    - Fiber: 1g

CHAPTER 8

GROCERY SHOPPING GUIDE

Adhering to a Blood Type O diet involves making mindful choices during grocery shopping. Here are some tips to help you navigate the aisles and make informed decisions:

1. Prioritize Whole Foods:

- Emphasize whole, unprocessed foods such as lean meats, fish, fruits, and vegetables. These are generally well-suited for a Blood Type O diet and provide essential nutrients.

2. Choose Quality Protein:

- Opt for lean, high-quality proteins like grass-fed beef, poultry, fish, and eggs. These can be central to a Blood Type O diet, providing necessary amino acids.

3. Include Beneficial Vegetables:

- Select a variety of vegetables, focusing on options like spinach, kale, broccoli, and Brussels sprouts. These vegetables are often recommended for Blood Type O individuals.

4. Limit Grains and Dairy:

- Minimize or avoid products containing wheat, corn, and dairy. Explore alternatives like almond or coconut milk, and consider grains like quinoa or rice in moderation.

5. Read Food Labels:

- Pay close attention to food labels. Look for hidden sources of ingredients that may not align with the Blood Type O diet, such as certain additives, preservatives, or non-compliant grains.

6. Choose Wild-Caught Fish:

- When selecting fish, prioritize wild-caught options over farm-raised. Wild-caught fish may offer a better nutrient profile and be a healthier choice for Blood Type O individuals.

7. Shop for Fresh Produce:

- Frequent the fresh produce section for a variety of fruits and vegetables. Opt for in-season, local produce when possible for optimal freshness and nutritional value.

8. Consider Alternative Grains:

- Explore alternative grains like rice, quinoa, and millet. These grains can be more compatible with a Blood Type O diet compared to some traditional grains.

9. Be Mindful of Additives:

- Avoid processed foods with artificial additives, colors, and sweeteners. These can have ingredients that may not align with the Blood Type O diet philosophy.

10. Plan and Prepare:

- Plan your meals ahead of time and create a shopping list. This helps you stay focused on purchasing items that are in line with the Blood Type O recommendations.

Reading Food Labels: Key Considerations:

1. Ingredients List:

- Check the ingredients list for any non-compliant items. Be cautious of hidden sources of wheat, corn, and dairy.

2. Nutritional Information:

- Review the nutritional information to ensure that the product aligns with the macronutrient recommendations for a Blood Type O diet.

3. Allergen Information:

- Verify the allergen information to identify any potential allergens that may need to be avoided based on your specific dietary needs.

4. Serving Size:

- Pay attention to the serving size. Adjust the nutritional values based on your intended portion size to get an accurate representation of the food's impact on your diet.

5. Certification Labels:

- Look for certification labels like "Non-GMO" or "Organic" to ensure a higher quality of the product.

IF YOU WANT MORE RECIPES, YOU CAN CHECK OUT OTHER BOOKS BY THE AUTHOR

GLUTEN-FREE INSTANT POT COOKBOOK

GLUTEN-FREE AIR FRYER COOKBOOK

GLUTEN-FREE SLOW COOKER COOKBOOK

MEDITERRANEAN DIET COOKBOOK FOR NEWBIES 2024

LOW SODIUM COOKBOOK FOR BEGINNERS

TO GET ACCESS TO MORE BOOKS BY THE AUTHOR SCAN THE QR CODE

CONCLUSION

As we reach the final pages of this culinary odyssey, I find myself filled with a profound sense of gratitude and hope. The journey we've shared, exploring the intricacies of the blood type O food list, has been more than a mere collection of recipes; it's been a celebration of life, health, and the transformative power of conscious choices.

In concluding our time together, I urge you to embrace the knowledge you've gained within these pages. Let it be a guiding light as you navigate the vast landscape of food choices, turning each meal into a symphony that harmonizes with the rhythm of your unique biology.

Remember, dear reader, that the power to nurture your well-being lies within you. The food you choose to put on your plate is not just sustenance; it's a gesture of self-love, a commitment to a life filled with vitality and joy.

As you embark on this journey beyond the book's cover, I encourage you to reflect on the changes you've witnessed within yourself. Notice the subtle shifts in energy, the newfound vibrancy in your step, and the enhanced connection between body and spirit. This is the magic of aligning your diet with the wisdom encoded in your blood type.

But our journey doesn't end here; it merely transforms into a shared exploration. Your feedback, your experiences, and your insights are invaluable. I invite you to reach out and share your stories, your challenges, and your triumphs. Your journey is unique, and by sharing it, you contribute to a tapestry of inspiration that can uplift others.

I'm not just Lorene Peachey, the nutritionist; I am a fellow traveler on this path to wellness. Your feedback is not just a collection of words; it's a connection, a conversation that extends beyond these pages. Let us continue this dialogue, supporting one another as we navigate the ever-evolving landscape of health and happiness.

Whether it's a tantalizing recipe that became a staple in your kitchen or a profound realization about the impact of blood type nutrition on your life, I want to hear from you. Your insights could be the spark that ignites a positive change in someone else's journey.

As you step forward, armed with newfound knowledge and a heart full of possibilities, know that you are not alone. The path to well-being is a shared endeavor, and I am honored to have walked a part of it with you.

In closing, I extend my heartfelt gratitude for embarking on this adventure with me. May your days be filled with delicious, nourishing meals and may your life be a testament to the incredible potential that lies within when we choose to honor our bodies and souls.

Wishing you a future filled with health, joy, and the boundless possibilities that come with a plate full of mindful choices.

BONUS CHAPTER 1

HEALTHY BLOOD TYPE O

RECIPES

Grilled Salmon with Lemon and Herbs

- **Cooking Time:** 15 minutes
- **Servings:** 4

Ingredients:

- 4 salmon fillets
- 2 tablespoons olive oil
- 1 lemon (juiced)
- 1 tablespoon fresh dill (chopped)
- Salt and pepper to taste

Instructions:

1. Preheat the grill to medium-high heat.

2. Brush salmon fillets with olive oil and lemon juice. Sprinkle with chopped dill, salt, and pepper.

3. Grill salmon for 5-7 minutes per side or until cooked through.

4. Serve with steamed vegetables.

Nutritional Information: 250 calories, 28g protein, 15g fat, 2g carbohydrates.

Quinoa and Vegetable Stir-Fry

- **Cooking Time:** 20 minutes

- **Servings:** 6

Ingredients:

- 2 cups cooked quinoa

- 1 cup broccoli florets

- 1 bell pepper (sliced)

- 1 zucchini (sliced)

- 1 cup snap peas

- 2 tablespoons soy sauce

- 1 tablespoon sesame oil

Instructions:

1. In a large pan, sauté vegetables in sesame oil until tender-crisp.

2. Add cooked quinoa to the pan and stir.

3. Drizzle with soy sauce and toss until well combined.

Nutritional Information: 220 calories, 8g protein, 8g fat, 30g carbohydrates.

Turkey and Vegetable Skewers

- **Cooking Time:** 25 minutes
- **Servings:** 4

Ingredients:

- 1 pound turkey breast (cut into cubes)
- 1 red onion (sliced)
- 1 bell pepper (sliced)
- 1 zucchini (sliced)
- 2 tablespoons olive oil
- 1 teaspoon dried oregano

Instructions:

1. Preheat the grill or oven.
2. Thread turkey and vegetables onto skewers.
3. Mix olive oil, oregano, salt, and pepper. Brush over skewers.
4. Grill or bake for 15-20 minutes, turning occasionally.

Nutritional Information: 280 calories, 30g protein, 10g fat, 15g carbohydrates.

Spinach and Mushroom Omelette

- **Cooking Time:** 10 minutes

- **Servings:** 2

Ingredients:

- 4 eggs

- 1 cup spinach (chopped)

- 1/2 cup mushrooms (sliced)

- 1/4 cup feta cheese (crumbled)

- Salt and pepper to taste

Instructions:

1. Whisk eggs in a bowl and season with salt and pepper.

2. In a non-stick pan, sauté mushrooms and spinach until wilted.

3. Pour whisked eggs over vegetables and cook until set.

4. Sprinkle with feta and fold the omelette in half.

Nutritional Information: 320 calories, 20g protein, 24g fat, 6g carbohydrates.

Chicken and Vegetable Stir-Fry with Cashews

- **Cooking Time:** 25 minutes

- **Servings:** 4

Ingredients:

- 1 pound chicken breast (sliced)

- 2 cups broccoli florets

- 1 red bell pepper (sliced)

- 1 cup snow peas

- 1/2 cup cashews

- 3 tablespoons soy sauce

- 1 tablespoon honey

- 1 tablespoon sesame oil

Instructions:

1. In a wok or large pan, stir-fry chicken until cooked.

2. Add vegetables and stir-fry until tender-crisp.

3. Mix soy sauce, honey, and sesame oil. Pour over the stir-fry.

4. Toss in cashews and cook for an additional 2 minutes.

Nutritional Information: 280 calories, 25g protein, 14g fat, 15g carbohydrates.

Greek Salad with Grilled Chicken

- **Cooking Time:** 20 minutes

- **Servings:** 4

Ingredients:

- 1 pound chicken thighs (boneless, skinless)
- 4 cups mixed greens
- 1 cucumber (sliced)
- 1 cup cherry tomatoes (halved)
- 1/2 red onion (thinly sliced)
- Feta cheese (crumbled)
- Greek dressing

Instructions:

1. Grill chicken until fully cooked.

2. Slice grilled chicken into strips.

3. In a large bowl, combine mixed greens, cucumber, tomatoes, and red onion.

4. Top with grilled chicken and feta cheese. Drizzle with Greek dressing.

Nutritional Information: 320 calories, 25g protein, 15g fat, 20g carbohydrates.

Baked Sweet Potato Fries

- **Cooking Time:** 30 minutes

- **Servings:** 4

Ingredients:

- 2 large sweet potatoes (cut into fries)

- 2 tablespoons olive oil

- 1 teaspoon paprika

- Salt and pepper to taste

Instructions:

1. Preheat the oven to 425°F (220°C).

2. In a bowl, toss sweet potato fries with olive oil, paprika, salt, and pepper.

3. Spread fries on a baking sheet in a single layer.

4. Bake for 25-30 minutes, turning halfway through.

Nutritional Information: 180 calories, 2g protein, 8g fat, 27g carbohydrates.

Shrimp and Avocado Salad

- **Cooking Time:** 15 minutes

- **Servings:** 2

Ingredients:

- 1/2 pound shrimp (peeled and deveined)

- 2 avocados (sliced)

- 1 cup cherry tomatoes (halved)

- 1/4 cup red onion (finely chopped)

- Fresh cilantro (chopped)

- Lime dressing (lime juice, olive oil, salt)

Instructions:

1. Sauté shrimp until pink and opaque.

2. In a bowl, combine shrimp, avocados, tomatoes, and red onion.

3. Drizzle with lime dressing and garnish with cilantro.

Nutritional Information: 280 calories, 20g protein, 18g fat, 15g carbohydrates.

9. Turkey and Vegetable Chili

- **Cooking Time:** 40 minutes
- **Servings:** 6

Ingredients:

- 1 pound ground turkey
- 1 onion (chopped)
- 2 bell peppers (chopped)
- 2 cans diced tomatoes (low sodium)
- 2 cans kidney beans (rinsed and drained)
- 2 tablespoons chili powder
- 1 teaspoon cumin

Instructions:

1. In a large pot, brown turkey with chopped onions.
2. Add bell peppers, diced tomatoes, kidney beans, chili powder, cumin, salt, and pepper.
3. Simmer for 30 minutes, stirring occasionally.

Nutritional Information: 280 calories, 20g protein, 8g fat, 35g carbohydrates.

10. Berry and Banana Smoothie Bowl

- **Preparation Time:** 10 minutes

- **Servings:** 2

Ingredients:

- 1 cup mixed berries (frozen)

- 2 bananas (sliced)

- 1 cup Greek yogurt

- 1 tablespoon chia seeds

- 2 tablespoons almond butter

- Granola for topping

Instructions:

1. Blend mixed berries, bananas, Greek yogurt, chia seeds, and almond butter until smooth.

2. Pour into bowls and top with granola.

Nutritional Information: 220 calories, 10g protein, 8g fat, 30g carbohydrates.

BONUS CHAPTER 2

EXERCISE RECOMMENDATION

Exercise is a vital component of maintaining overall health and well-being. When it comes to individuals with Blood Type O, there are certain exercise recommendations that align with the principles of the Blood Type Diet. While it's important to note that individual preferences, fitness levels, and health conditions play a significant role in determining the most suitable exercise routine, understanding the general guidelines can provide a helpful starting point.

1. Emphasis on Intense Physical Activity:

Blood Type O individuals are often described as having a naturally robust and resilient constitution, which may be well-suited for more intense physical activities. Engaging in activities that raise the heart rate and promote cardiovascular health is beneficial. This can include activities like high-intensity interval training (HIIT), running, and strength training.

2. Aerobic Exercises:

Aerobic exercises play a crucial role in supporting cardiovascular health. Blood Type O individuals may benefit from activities that enhance endurance and stamina. These exercises can include running, cycling, swimming, and brisk walking. Aim for at least 150 minutes of moderate-intensity aerobic exercise per week, as recommended by health authorities.

3. Strength Training:

Incorporating strength training exercises is essential for building and maintaining muscle mass, which can contribute to a strong and lean physique. Focus on compound exercises such as squats, deadlifts, and bench presses. Aim for at least two days of strength training per week, targeting major muscle groups.

4. Interval Training:

High-intensity interval training (HIIT) can be particularly effective for Blood Type O individuals. This involves alternating short bursts of intense activity with periods of rest. HIIT not only improves cardiovascular health but also enhances metabolism and promotes fat loss.

5. Outdoor Activities:

Given the energetic and outdoorsy nature associated with Blood Type O, incorporating outdoor activities can be highly enjoyable. Activities such as hiking, trail running, or participating in team sports not only provide physical benefits but also contribute to mental well-being.

6. Mind-Body Exercises:

Mind-body exercises, such as yoga and tai chi, can be valuable additions to the exercise routine for Blood Type O individuals. These activities promote flexibility, balance, and stress reduction. Yoga offers various styles, including power yoga or vinyasa, which can align with the dynamic nature of Blood Type O.

7. Individual Preferences Matter:

While general recommendations are valuable, individual preferences play a crucial role in sustaining a regular exercise routine. Blood Type O individuals are encouraged to explore various activities and find those that resonate with their interests, ensuring long-term adherence to a healthy and active lifestyle.

8. Precautions and Consultation:

Before starting any new exercise regimen, it is advisable for individuals, regardless of blood type, to consult with a healthcare professional or fitness expert. This is especially important for those with existing health conditions or individuals who have been relatively inactive. A personalized approach to exercise takes into account individual health status, fitness levels, and goals.

9. Consistency is Key:

Consistency is a fundamental aspect of any successful fitness journey. Blood Type O individuals should strive to make exercise a regular part of their routine. This not only maximizes the benefits but also fosters a sense of discipline and well-being.

10. Listen to Your Body:

Lastly, it's crucial for individuals to listen to their bodies. Blood Type O individuals may find that their bodies respond differently to various types of exercise. Pay attention to how the body feels during and after activities and make adjustments accordingly. Rest and recovery are integral parts of any well-rounded fitness plan.

Printed in Great Britain
by Amazon